Sunshine 3

Pupil's Book

Erarbeitet von
Inga Bensmann (Weyhe)
Bianca Bläser (Merzenich)
Helga Haudeck (Ludwigsburg)
Daniela Röbers (Erkelenz)
Caroline Schröder (München)
Maria Sussex (Frankfurt am Main)

Unter Einbeziehung der Ausgabe von
Tanja Beattie
Inga Bensmann
Helga Haudeck
Birgit Hollbrügge
Stefanie Keller
Nadine Kerler
Ulrike Kraaz
Caroline Schröder

Cornelsen

Contents

- listen to your partner / teacher
- listen to the audio
- talk
- read
- write
- mediation
- colour, draw
- point
- play (a game)
- act out
- choice
- media
- ① easy
- ② medium
- ③ difficult
- extra

1 Talk about the picture.

2 Read the words and find the pictures: computer, cowboy, hamburger, laptop, skateboard, cap, ball.

- Aufg. 1: auch Einwortsätze als sprachliche Leistung akzeptieren
- Aufg. 1: *there's / there are* für die Bildbeschreibung nutzen

p. 3 APP

Getting started

6 ① Listen to the rhyme. Point to the pictures.

② Say the rhyme with a partner.

③ Say the rhyme and do the actions.

Do you know more numbers? Say the numbers. Write the numbers. Work with a partner.

APP p. 5

Aufg. 3: ggf. nur die Bewegungen ausführen

(1) Talk about the picture.

(2) Listen. Point to the pictures. 7

What is Mr Mole dreaming about?

There's a sandwich.

There are two balls.

(3) Listen and point. 8

(4) Read the texts.

Find out more about moles on the internet. Make a poster.

Note
Type in "Maulwurf" or "Maulwurfshügel".

Moles live **underground**.

Moles make **molehills**.

Moles are **black** and almost **blind**.

Moles eat **worms**.

Aufg. Sonne (o.): Global- / Detailverstehen der Geschichte erfragen
Aufg. Sonne (u.): altersangemessene Suchmaschinen nutzen

1 Meeting friends

1 Talk about the picture.

2 Listen. Point to the numbers.

3 Listen. Say the colours.

4 Listen. Where do Samir, Harry, Kate and Emily live? 12

What do you know about England?
Think. → Pair. → Share.

Note
In Großbritannien sind alle Briefkästen rot. Fallen dir weitere Besonderheiten auf?

APP p. 7, 9

Aufg. 1: zum Sprechen im ganzen Satz ermutigen
ggf. Erklärfilm *Pronouns*

1 Listen. Point to the numbers.

2 Read and say the numbers.

3 Play 'hopscotch'.

4 Explain.

5 Read the dialogue with a partner.

Walk and talk.

Aufg. 2: Möglichkeit zum Zählen in den Familiensprachen der Kinder nutzen
Aufg. Sonne: ggf. KV *Walk and talk* nutzen

p. 8, 9 APP

Meeting friends

1 Talk about Harry's family.

This is Harry's ...

Number ... is Harry's ...

13 **2 Listen. Point to the pictures.**

I'm 9 years old. How old are you?

3 Read and look at Harry's family. Say the numbers.

I'm Harry's uncle. Harry's father is my brother.

Hello. I'm Harry's aunt. My name is Djamila.

I'm 6 years old. Harry is my older brother. My name is Luke.

Hi. We are Harry's cousins. We are twins.

That's number ...

APP p. 10

Aufg. 1: evtl. verschiedene Familienkonstellationen thematisieren

Let's talk

1. Read the dialogues. Talk to a partner.
2. Make up your own dialogue.
- Walk and talk.

Aufg. 1: untere Szene = anspruchsvollerer Erweiterungsdialog
Aufg. Sonne: ggf. KV *Walk and talk* nutzen

p. 12 APP

Media: How to take a photo

1. Read the texts.
2. Explain.
3. Search for things in your favourite colour. Take photos of them.

Make posters for each colour. Present.

Note
Achte darauf, dass Fotos von dir und deiner Familie nicht ins Internet gelangen.

① 
Take a tablet or a smartphone.

② 
Find the camera app.

③ 
Find things in your favourite colour.

④ 
Take photos.

p. 12

Aufg. 3: Gegenstände beispielhaft zur Verfügung stellen

More to explore: Colours and flags

① Where do they speak English? Talk.

Listen to your partner. Point to the country.

② Find more countries with English as an official language.

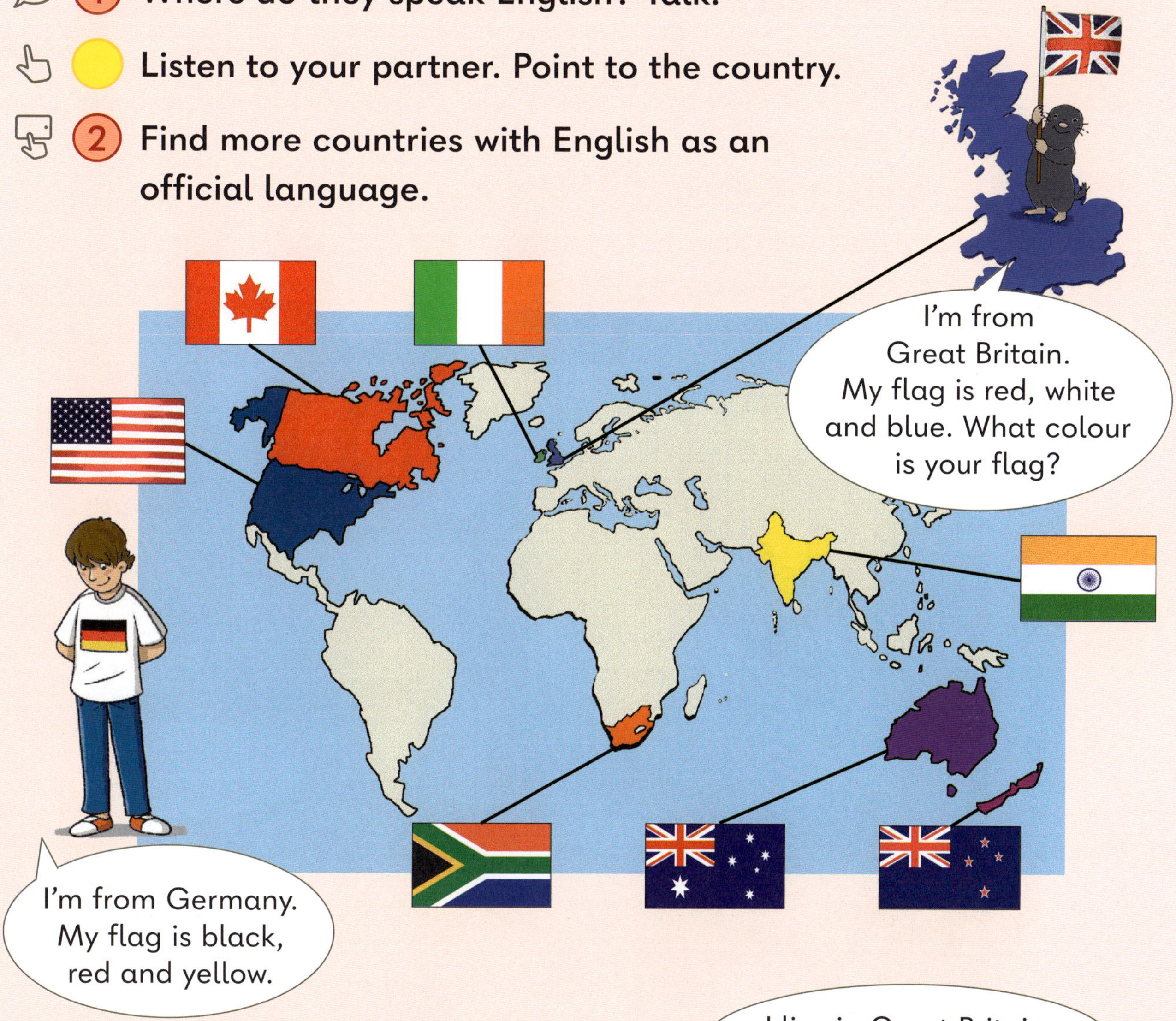

What about you? Talk.

I'm from …
My family is from …
My aunt / uncle / … lives in …

Aufg. 1: weitere englischsprachige Länder suchen und benennen
Aufg. 2: Tipps für kindgerechte Suchmaschinen und geeignete Suchbegriffe (z. B. *English official language*) geben

p. 64 APP

2 Pets in the garden

① Talk about the picture.

There's a cat. The cat is black and white.

There are ...

② Listen. What pets have the children got? 23

What other pets do you know? Find more words.

Think. → Pair. → Share.

APP p. 17

Aufg. 1: Erklärfilm *There's ... / There are ...*

Aufg. 2: Sätze mit *a / the* formulieren: *Emily has got a cat. The cat is black and white.*

1 Talk about the picture.

2 Listen. Who is on the telephone?

22

Note

People drink a lot of tea in Britain.

3 Read. Which pet is it? Find out.

① The pet is green, blue or yellow. It can sing.	
② The pet is brown, black or white. It likes carrots and lettuce.	
③ The pet is grey or white. It likes cheese.	
④ The pet is brown. Its favourite food is lettuce.	

4 Talk and listen to your partner. What pet is it?

Aufg. 1: traditioneller *Afternoon Tea* zwischen drei und fünf Uhr am Nachmittag, daher auch als *Five-o-Clock-Tea* bezeichnet

p. 17, 18 APP

Pets in the garden

Let's talk

1. Read the dialogues. Talk to a partner.
2. Make up your own dialogue.

Walk and talk.

Aufg. 1: untere Szene = anspruchsvollerer Erweiterungsdialog
Aufg. Sonne: ggf. KV *Walk and talk* nutzen

Story: Rabbit's party

25 (1) Listen to the story.

(2) Read the story.

(3) Act out the story.

Write a party invitation.

Aufg. Sonne: ggf. Einladungen zu anderen Partys anregen
abschließend gemeinsam den Film zur Story anschauen

p. 19 APP

2 Pets in the garden

1 Read the words and sentences.

2 Explain.

3 Play the game.

	Take a card. Say a sentence.	carrot	Go to the matching picture.
	Go 3 steps forward.		Go to the matching word.
	Go back.		Miss a turn.

p. 17

- Aufg. 3: englische Spielanweisungen nutzen: *It's my / your turn; Roll the dice; Go … steps forward / backward.*
- Aufg. 3: Spielanweisungen optional auf Deutsch sagen

Media: How to record an audio or a video

1. Read the texts.
2. Explain.
3. Introduce yourself.

Note
Wenn du nicht gefilmt werden willst, ist eine Audio-Aufnahme oft eine gute Alternative.

① 

Choose the voice record icon or the camera icon.

② 

Press the record button.

③ 

Introduce yourself and record it.

19

4. Listen to the rap.
5. Do the rap and record it.

Can I have a dog, Mum?
Can I have a dog?
I really want a dog, Mum.
Please let me have a dog!

Kate's got a hamster, Mum.
Emily's got a cat.
Samir's got a guinea pig.
(Mum: And you've got a rabbit and a rat!)

But I want a dog, Mum.
I really want a dog.
Can I have a dog, Mum?
Please let me have a dog!

Aufg. 5: auf Betonung und Sprechgeschwindigkeit achten; ggf. einzelne Textpassagen sprechen lassen

p. 15 APP

More to explore: Dogs

1 Listen and point to the pictures.

29

1

sheep dog

2

rescue dog

3

police dog

4
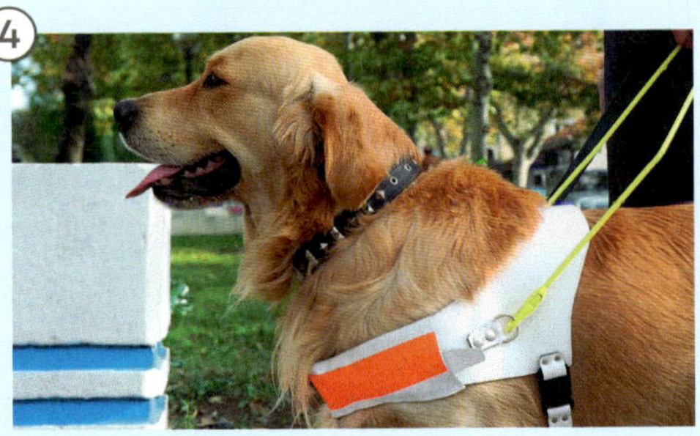
guide dog

2 Read the speech bubbles with a partner.

3 Do the dog actions with your partner. Guess the actions. Take turns.

4 Explain.

APP

das Material zum fächerübergreifenden Lernen (*Arts and crafts: Making a felt dog*, s. HRU) nutzen

At school

① Talk about the picture.

33 ② Listen to the song. Point to the school things in the picture.

Where are the school things? Write sentences.

The chair is next to the table.

Think. → Pair. → Share.

Where's Mr Mole?
Where can he be?
Where's Mr Mole?
Let me see.

Is he in the school bag?
Is he on the book?
Or under the table?
Let's have a look.

No! Not there!

Note

In Großbritannien gibt es in vielen Klassen einen zweiten Lehrer oder eine zweite Lehrerin. Diese Person nennt man *classroom assistant*.

Aufg. 1: *there's / there are* für die Bildbeschreibung nutzen

p. 25 APP

3 At school

1 **Where are the school things? Choose one picture. Talk to a partner.**

The book is behind the door.
The lunch box is ...
Which picture is it?

It's picture B.

A

B

C

D

Talk to a partner. Listen and do.

Put the scissors on the table.

Let's put the worms in my lunch box. Yummy!

p. 25

Aufg. 1: Partnerkinder wechseln, um die Übung zu vertiefen

① Read the texts (1–5).

② Explain.

③ Play the game in groups of four.

④ Explain the rules. Record a video or an audio.

① Take these five cards from your word box.

② Put your cards on the table.

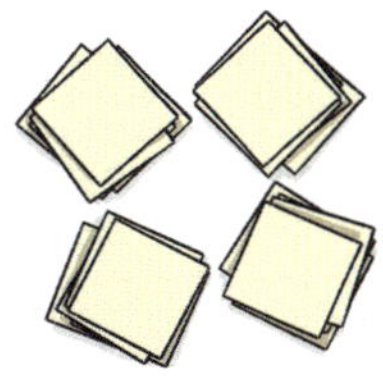

③ Shuffle all the cards.

④ Give five cards to each player.

⑤ Ask questions.
The player with the most cards wins.

Aufg. 3: Redemittel nutzen, um unabhängig vom Spiel nach Gegenständen bzw. Minibildkarten zu fragen

3 At school

Let's talk

(1) Read the dialogues. Talk to a partner.

(2) Make up your own dialogue.

Walk and talk.

36 (3) Listen and read.

(4) Say the tongue twisters.

Record a tongue twister. or Draw pictures.

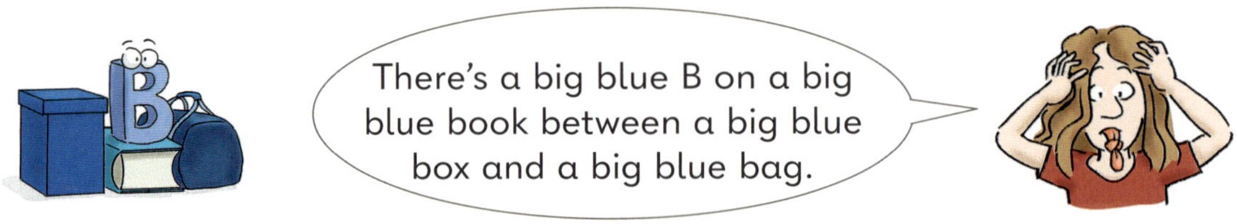

Peter picked a purple pen from Penny's pink pencil case.

Seven silly pairs of scissors are sitting on a chair.

- Aufg. Sonne (o.): ggf. KV *Walk and talk* nutzen
- Aufg. 4: Zungenbrecher in unterschiedlichen Geschwindigkeiten aufsagen lassen
- Aufg. Sonne (u.): Internet-Recherche nach weiteren Zungenbrechern

Story: Jack's bad day

37 ① Listen to the story.

② Read the story.

③ What happens in the end?

Think. → Pair. → Share.

weiterführend ein Rollenspiel (*Act out the story*) durchführen
abschließend gemeinsam den Film zur Story anschauen

More to explore: School in Britain

Note

In Großbritannien schaust du zuerst nach rechts, wenn du eine Straße überquerst. Weißt du, warum?

(1) **Talk about the pictures.**

40 (2) **Listen. Point to the pictures.**

(3) **Read the texts.**

① 

A **lollipop man** helps children cross the road.

② 

Some children walk to school with the **walking bus**.

③ 

This is a **school building**.

④ 

School starts with **assembly**.

(4) **Make a school badge.**

You need:

cardboard

felt tips or coloured pencils

scissors

a safety pin

sticky tape

① Draw a circle on the cardboard. Write the name of your school. Colour the badge.

② Cut out the badge.

③ Tape a safety pin to the back of your badge.

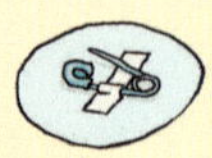

(5) **Explain.**

das Material zum fächerübergreifenden Lernen (*Printing your own school T-shirt*, s. HRU) nutzen

More to explore: Eco learning at school

41

① **Listen. Point to the pictures.**

② **Where are the children from? Read the texts.**

③ **What do the children do to protect nature? Explain.**

1

Hi, we are from India. For our school play, we are dressing up like wild animals. Many of them are in danger. Do you like our costumes?

2

Hello, we are from South Africa.
We recycle paper, glass and plastic.
No plastic is fantastic!

3

Hello, I'm from China. For our Low Carbon Day we are painting eco-friendly bags. Do you like my drawing?

4

Hi, there. We are from the USA.
We love our vertical school garden!

5

Hi, we are from England. Here we are working in our new school garden. It's fun!

What can you and your school do to protect nature?
Think. → Pair. → Share.

recyle • refill • repair • reuse

Aufg. 1: anhand länderspezifischer Akzente in den Hörtexten für die Bedeutung des Englischen als *global language* sensibilisieren

p. 60

How to learn new words

Look at the methods.
Try them out!

Make a mind map

1

① Choose a topic for your mind map.
② Write down all the words and sentences you know.
③ Look up new words in a dictionary.
④ Draw pictures for your words.

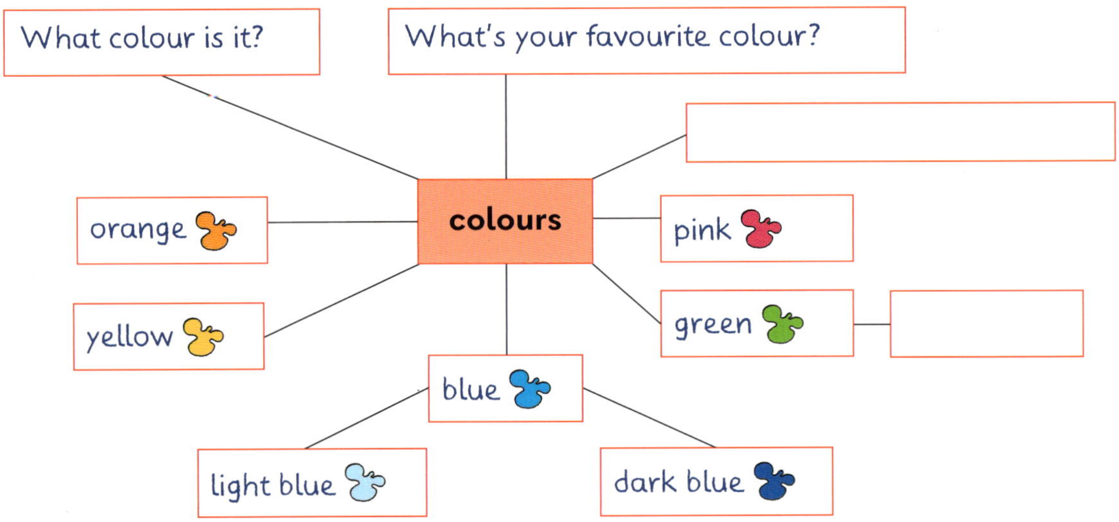

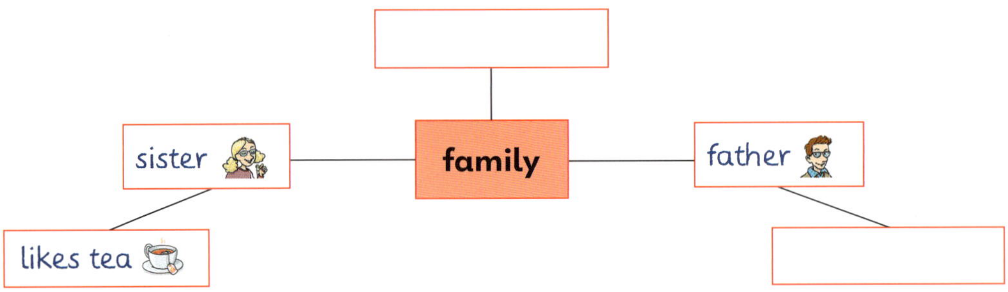

Make a mind map on your computer. Take photos.

p. 79

- Einschätzung zu jeder Methode ins *Pocket book* (s. *Activity Book*) eintragen
- ggf. KV *Mind map* zur Verfügung stellen
- Aufg. 2: Wörter, Satzbausteine, Frage- und Antwortsätze sind möglich

How to learn new words

Write, draw and look

1

① Write English words on sheets of paper.
Draw or cut out and glue pictures.

② Tape the papers around your room or your house (if your parents agree).

③ Look at the words and pictures every day.

bike

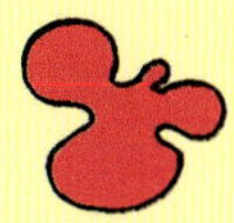

pink

Pick a pair

2

① Make mini picture cards:
Cut out cardboard.
Write an English word on one card.
Draw a matching picture on a second card.

② Play pick a pair.

guinea pig

Aufg. 1 (Unit 2): Rückseite der Kärtchen markieren, um Selbstkontrolle zu ermöglichen
Aufg. 2 (Unit 2): Spielregeln wiederholen; auf Besonderheiten hinweisen

p. 79

How to learn new words

Talk and move

2

① Read the English words or sentences.
② Say the words and move.

Record the words. Listen. Say the words and move.

Write and label

3

① Write English words on sticky notes.
② Label things or pictures.

Take photos and print them out. Label the photos.

p. 79

Aufg. 1 (Unit 3): Klebezettel zur Verfügung stellen

Record and listen

3

① Take your word list (p. 64). Read the words.
Record them.

② Take your mini picture cards. Listen and do a "listening line".

Are you a listening expert? Make your own word cards.
Listen and do a "reading line".

pencil | rubber | scissors | pencil case | glue stick | ruler

Rate the methods

① Look at your pocket book (Activity Book, p. 79).
Rate the methods.
Let the sun shine!

② Which method is your favourite?
What helps you best to learn new words?

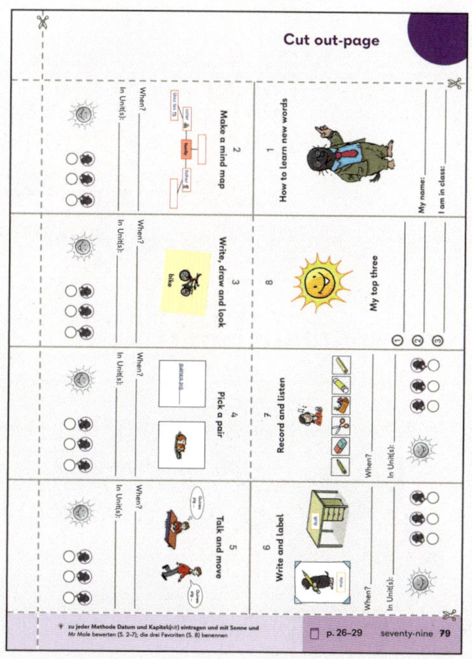

Aufg. 1: nur Wörter, die auch als Bildkarte vorhanden sind, einsetzen
Aufg. Sonne: Wörter aufnehmen, anhören und passende Karten legen
Aufg. 1, 2 (u.): *Pocket book* dient individueller Bewertung der Methoden

p. 79

4 The second-hand shop

1 Talk about the picture.

There's ...

There are ...

2 Listen to your partner. Point.

3 What is in the shop? Make a list.
Think. → Pair. → Share.

There is	a	pink hat.
There are		hats.

Play "I spy". Explain the rules.

Note
There is **a pair of** jeans.
There are jeans.

APP p. 32

- Aufg. 3: zur Unterstützung mit der *Word list* (s. S. 65–66) arbeiten lassen
- Aufg. Sonne: *I spy (with my little eye) something brown / ... – Is it ...?*
- Aufg. Sonne: Sozialformen variieren (Partner / Gruppe / Plenum)

The second-hand shop

1 Listen to your teacher. Who is it?

2 Choose one picture. Talk to a partner.

She's wearing a dress. The dress is red. Who is it?

It's ...

What is Samir wearing? Write.

He is wearing…

Note

she (girl) he (boy)

1

Sarah

2

Harry

3

Kate

4

Samir

5

Emily

6

John

Aufg. 1: genaue Anzahl (*a* / *2* / *5* / ...) oder allg. Formulierung *some* verwenden: *She's wearing a purple hat.* / *She's wearing two* / *some white socks.*
Erklärfilm *pronouns*

p. 31 APP

The second-hand shop

Let's talk

1. Read the dialogues. Talk to a partner.
2. Make up your own dialogue.

Walk and talk.

- Aufg. 1: Szenen 2–4 = anspruchsvollere Erweiterungsdialoge
- Aufg. 1 u. 2: Vertiefung der Struktur *What about …?* in Unit 5
- Aufg. Sonne: ggf. KV *Walk and talk* nutzen

1 Read and point to the pictures.

(A)

1 I'm Joseph. This is my favourite outfit: colourful trousers, my red shirt and my green hat. I don't like shoes!

3 I'm Oscar. I'm wearing my black boots, grey trousers and my blue and red jacket. Do you like my orange cap?

(B)

(C)

2 My name is Eliza. I'm wearing blue shorts, my orange T-shirt and my brown sandals. That's my favourite outfit!

4 My name is Ruby. I'm wearing my favourite pink socks, my yellow shirt and my purple skirt. I love my white trainers!

(D)

2 What are the children wearing? Talk.

Hannah is wearing...

Layla

Tom

Samuel

Hannah

3 Talk about the outfits.

Too cold, too warm, or perfect? Why?

I think ... is wearing a perfect outfit because ...

...'s outfit is not perfect because ...

4 Look at the outfits. Give advice.

Take off your ...! / Put on your ...!

- Aufg. 1: Lesen durch Tandemlesen vorentlasten
- Aufg. 2: zusätzlich Sätze schreiben lassen (*Tom is wearing* ...); über das Lieblingsoutfit sprechen lassen (*My favourite outfit is* ... *because* ...)

p. 31 APP

The second-hand shop

Media: How to find information on a website

1. Look at the website dictionary. Find the words on the website.
2. Listen and point.

- Find more information on the internet. Type in “Scotland”, “kilt”, “tartan”. Design a website.

Note

Im Internet werden dir oft Dinge zum Kauf angeboten. Stimme dem nie zu und klicke keine Links an.

Website dictionary

help	Here you find tips on how to use the website.
contact	Here you often find an email address, a phone number or a map.
FAQ	Here you find answers to many questions. (FAQ = frequently asked questions)
menu	Here you see what you can find on the website.
search	Here you can type in what you are looking for.

Aufg. 1: ggf. weitere Begriffe finden lassen

Aufg. 2: Dinge benennen, die auf der Seite zu sehen sind (z. B. *kilt*, *hat*, *socks*); fächerübergreifendes Lernen: einen Tartan entwerfen / einen Kilt nähen

Story: A funny boy

1 **Read the story.**

2 **Act out the story.**

3 **Dress up and make a video.**
or **Draw and record an audio.**

Note
Wenn du nicht gefilmt werden möchtest, kannst du auch Stabpuppen basteln und die Geschichte nachspielen.

Aufg. 3: ggf. Kamishibai (japanisches Erzähltheater, s. HRU)
abschließend gemeinsam den Film zur Story anschauen
ggf. das Audio zur Story vorspielen (Track 48)

Story: The smartest giant in town

50 ① Listen to the story. Point to the pictures.

② Talk about the pictures. How does the story end?

Read the rhyme with a partner. Point to the pictures.
What about picture 6?

My tie is a scarf for a cold giraffe.
My shirt's on a boat as a sail for a goat.
My shoe is a house for a little white mouse.
One of my socks is a bed for a fox.
My belt helped a dog who was crossing a bog.

Note ⚠

Find the rhyming words:
boat – goat
...
Make a list.

Aufg. 1: die Geschichte im Rahmen eines *Storytellings* im Kinositz vor der Klasse präsentieren

More to explore: School uniforms

① Talk about school uniforms. What is the boy wearing? What is the girl wearing?

The girl is wearing …

a cardigan • a pullover • a shirt • shoes • a skirt • socks • a tie • trousers

Note

At some schools, boys and girls wear the same uniforms. The uniforms are unisex.

51 ② Listen. Point to the pictures.

③ Listen to your partner. Which school is it?

①

②

③

Queen's school

Blake school

Swanage school

In what other countries do children wear school uniforms? Do research.

5 Free-time activities

53 **1** Listen to the song. Point to the pictures.

2 Sing the song. **or** Do the actions.

Football, music, books, TV, bikes and comics, friends, PC. Tell me, tell me, what about you? Do you like the things I do?	Playing football is what I like. Watching TV, riding my bike.	Listening to music, tapping my feet, meeting friends in the street.	Reading books and comics, too. Playing computer games. What about you?

■ Aufg. 1: den Song mit passenden Bewegungen demonstrieren und ggf. in unterschiedlichen Geschwindigkeiten vorspielen

Let's talk

(1) Read the dialogues. Talk to a partner.

(2) Make up your own dialogue.

Walk and talk.

57 (3) Listen to the rap. Point to the pictures.

(4) Read.

Present the rap with a partner or in a group.

Where's the cat? Where's the cat?
Is it in the living room – watching TV?
Is it in the kitchen – drinking my tea?

Where's the cat? Where's the cat?
Is it in the bedroom – eating my shoe?
Is it in the bathroom – playing with shampoo?

Where's the cat? Where's the cat?
There it is – sleeping in Mum's favourite hat.

Aufg. 1: Szene 2 = anspruchsvollerer Erweiterungsdialog
Aufg. Sonne (o.): ggf. KV *Walk and talk* nutzen
Aufg. 3: den Rap in unterschiedlichen Geschwindigkeiten vorspielen

p. 41 APP

Media: How to make a podcast

1 What do you like doing in your free time? Record an audio podcast.

1

Plan your podcast in a group.

2

Start your podcast.

3

Play your welcome melody.

4

Present your guest.

5

Talk to your guest.

6

End your podcast.

p. 39, 40

Aufg. 1: Hilfe für Sprachproduktion anbieten (s. KV *Script* und KV *More ideas and help*); Rollenverteilung vorab besprechen und ggf., je nach Gruppenstärke, Rollen doppelt besetzen

① Talk about the picture.

② Where are the pets? Where are the children? Talk to a partner.

Where's the cat?

It's in the kitchen.

Where's Emily?

She's ...

What are the children and the pets doing? Write sentences.

Samir is playing … / The cat is …

Think. → Pair. → Share.

Aufg. 1: als Vorentlastung für Aufg. Sonne über gerade stattfindende Aktivitäten sprechen (*he / she / it is + …-ing, they are + …-ing*)

Aufg. Sonne: Beispielsätze im Singular und Plural geben

p. 41, 42 APP

Story: The babysitters

58 (1) Listen to the story. Point to the pictures.

(2) Read the story.

58 (3) Listen to the story. What do they not say?

Aufg. 2: Sprechblasen mit entsprechender Mimik vorlesen
abschließend gemeinsam den Film zur Story anschauen

Story: Aaaarrgghh, spider!

59 ① Listen and point.

② Talk.

③ Read the story.

④ How does the story end? Draw. or Act out.

① 

This is me. I'm a lonely spider.

② 

I want to be this family's pet, too. What can I do? None of their pets can dance like me!

③ 

None of their pets are clean like me!

④ 

None of their pets can feed themselves like I can!

⑤ 

⑥ 

⑦ 

⑧ ?

I am so happy! I think I'll show my family to all my friends ...

⑤ Find out more on the internet. Type in "spider", "facts", "kids".

Aufg. 2: nach Ort und Aktivitäten der Spinne fragen *(Where's the spider? What can it do?)*

p. 44

5 Free-time activities

① Where are the pets? Where is the spider? Talk.

The dog is between ...

② How can you take a spider out of the house? Read.

③ Explain.

Spiders are helpful! They eat bugs.

You need: cardboard | a glass or plastic box

What you do:

1. Open the door or window.

2. Place the glass over the spider.

3. Put the cardboard under the spider.

4. Take the spider out and set it free.

④ Listen to the song. Do the actions.

60

Incy Wincy Spider
went up the water spout,
down came the rain,
and washed the spider out.

Out came the sunshine
and dried up all the rain.
So Incy Wincy Spider
went up the spout again.

⑤ Go on the internet. Type in "Incy wincy spider around the world". Sing the song in other languages.

APP p. 44

Aufg. 1: die Abbildung zum Üben von Präpositionen nutzen
Aufg. 4: Song ähnelt einer kurzen Story, daher Formulierung im *Simple past*

More to explore: Games

1 Look at the pictures. Read the names of the games.

2 Listen. Point to the pictures. 63

3 Talk about the games.

Playground games

connect 4 • hide-and-seek • skipping • tag

4 Explain.

5 Play "rock, paper, scissors".

Note

Was spielst du gerne auf dem Schulhof? Vergleiche!

1 Say and do.

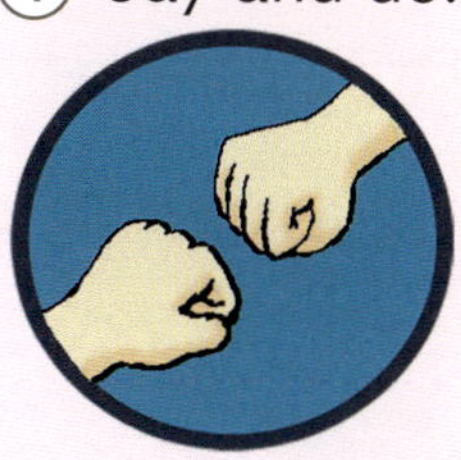

Rock, paper, scissors. Show!

2 Who is the winner?

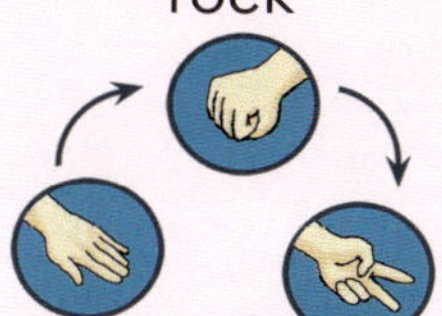

3 Two hands the same?

Play again!

In the park

(1) Talk about the picture.

There's ...

There are ...

(2) Listen to your teacher. Find the numbers. Point.

Talk to a partner. How many dogs / tables / scooters / ... can you see?

I can see ...

APP p. 47

- Aufg. 1: Aktivitäten ggf. durch Bewegungen vorspielen
- Aufg. 2: auch die Farbe der Zahlen benennen lassen

1 Talk about the picture.

How much is …? / How much are the …?

It's … / They're …

2 Listen. What does the boy say?

70

3 Read. Which shopping list is it?

I'm so hungry. I'd like one sandwich and two bananas.

I'd like a banana milk.

Phew, I'm hot. I need a nice cool drink. What about an orange juice and three oranges?

And ice cream for me, please! Chocolate, strawberry and vanilla are my favourites.

1
- 1 banana milk
- 1 sandwich
- 3 bananas
- 1 orange juice
- ice cream: vanilla, chocolate, cherry

2
- ice cream: chocolate, vanilla, strawberry
- 1 apple juice
- 1 sandwich
- 1 banana milk
- 2 bananas

3
- 1 orange juice
- 1 sandwich
- ice cream: chocolate, vanilla, strawberry
- 2 bananas
- 3 oranges
- 1 banana milk

4 Write your own shopping list. Be careful: you only have £ 3.50!

Think. → Pair. → Share.

Aufg. 1: darauf hinweisen, dass in GB nicht mit Euros und Cent bezahlt wird
Aufg. 4: ggf. ohne Geldlimit bearbeiten

p. 48, 51 APP

In the park

Let's talk

Note
You write: £ 1.50
You say: "One pound fifty"

1. Read the dialogues. Talk to a partner.
2. Make up your own dialogue.

Walk and talk.

Aufg. 1: Szenen 2–4 = anspruchsvollere Erweiterungsdialoge
Aufg. 2: jeweils einen Beispieldialog zur individuellen Bearbeitung nutzen
Aufg. Sonne: ggf. KV *Walk and talk* nutzen

1 Listen. Whose basket is it?

Ben • Leyla • Samantha • Tommy

2 Describe one of the baskets to your partner. What's in the basket?

Number ... is Ben's basket.

1

2

3

4

3 Explain the game "I packed my basket (and in it I put ...)".

I packed my basket and in it I put two apples.

I packed my basket and in it I put two apples and a kiwi smoothie.

I packed my basket and in it I put two apples, a kiwi smoothie and carrot sticks.

4 Play the game.

■ Aufg. 2: Korb 1 und 2 = etwas weniger umfangreich
▲ Aufg. 3 u. 4: Spiel beruht auf authentischen Satzstrukturen

p. 49, 50

Story: Where's my ice cream?

73 ① Listen to the story.

② Read the speech bubbles.

③ Say what is right and what is wrong.

APP

die Geschichte mit den *role cards* in Kleingruppen nachspielen

abschließend gemeinsam den Film zur Story anschauen

More to explore: Signs in the park

① Look at the signs. Read the sentences.

② Talk about the signs.

①

②

③

④

⑤

⑥

Wheelchair access

No dogs

No horse riding

No ball games

No bikes

Please keep off the grass

③ Find more signs.

Take photos and explain. or **Draw and explain.**

Aufg. 3: vielfältige Bearbeitungsmöglichkeiten: Fantasieschilder malen / gestalten, Schilder in der Umgebung finden und abzeichnen / fotografieren, im Internet nach Schildern forschen

p. 69 APP

More to explore: Kiwis and kiwis

1 Listen and point to the pictures.

77

1

2

3

4

2 Read the facts about kiwi fruits and point.

1. The kiwi fruit has its name because its skin looks like the feathers of the kiwi bird.
2. Kiwi plants grow like vines and can grow to 10 meters long.
3. Kiwis fly more than 18,000 km before we can eat them.
4. One kiwi has more vitamin C than two oranges.
5. There are more than 60 kinds of kiwis. The smallest is the kiwi berry.
6. Some people have allergies to kiwis.

A

B

C

D
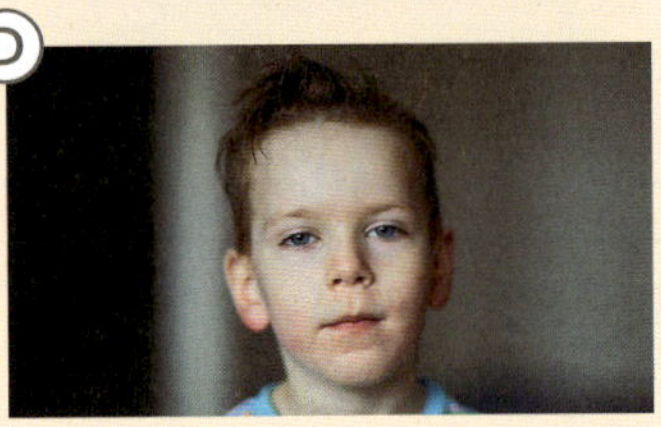

E

F

3 Make a kiwi smoothie. Read and explain.

You need: 2 kiwis, 1 banana, 100 ml orange juice

1. Peel and cut the kiwis and the banana.
2. Put them into the mixer.
3. Add the orange juice.
4. Mix and enjoy!

Aufg. 1 u. 2: ggf. Internet-Recherche über Kiwis anschließen
Aufg. 3: mit anderen Obstsorten / Säften variieren, optional mit Honig süßen

① Talk about the picture.

② Read.

③ Listen to the rap. Do the actions.

78/79

Birthday girl / boy – let's celebrate!
Birthday girl / boy – you are so great!
Birthday girl / boy – how old are you?
I'm 8 / 9 / ...!
1-2-3 – you're 8 / 9 / ... today!
1-2-3-4-5-6-7-8/-9/-...!
Happy birthday! **(3x)**
Hey!

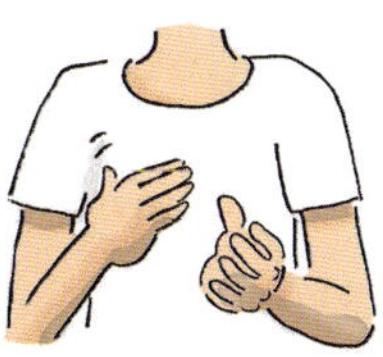

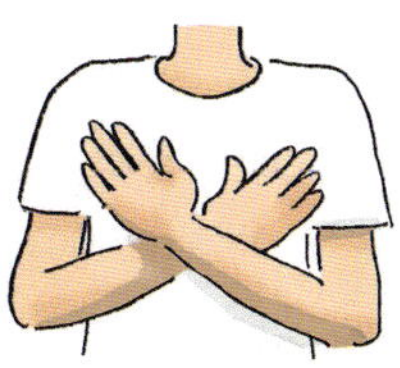

Note

Zum Geburtstag tragen englische Kinder gerne selbst gebastelte Hüte oder Kronen. Wie feierst du deinen Geburtstag?

Aufg. 3: ausführliche Anleitung für *Body percussion* zum Rap, s. HRU
Aufg. 3: Erklärfilm *Body percussion*

APP

Special days: Christmas

1 Look at the picture. Talk about the Christmas things.

Note
Kinder in Großbritannien hängen am 24.12. Strümpfe auf. Diese werden über Nacht gefüllt. Kennst du weitere Besonderheiten?

2 Look at the pictures. Find the Christmas things in the house.

Aufg. 1: *there's / there are* für die Bildbeschreibung nutzen
Aufg. 2: auch andere Gegenstände im Haus nennen und darauf zeigen lassen: *Point to …*

APP p. 57

Special days: Christmas

1 Talk about the pictures. Do you know these Christmas figures?

2 Who is it? Listen and point to the pictures. 85

① 
② 
③ 
④ 
⑤ 

Christkind • Father Christmas / Santa Claus •
Father Frost (Дед Мороз) • Hoteiosho • la Befana

3 Listen and talk. When do children get presents? In what country? Who is missing? 85

How do you celebrate in your family? Talk.

The name of our special day is ...
We celebrate on ...
We (do not) get presents.
We go to church / mosque / synagogue / ...
We stay at home. / We visit ...
We eat ...
...

Note
Not all families celebrate Christmas. There are many other religious and non-religious celebrations around the world.

4 What do these greetings mean? Find out!

I wish you a merry Christmas and a happy New Year!

Schana towa!

Feliz navidad!

Eid Mubarak!

Sretan Božić!

Aufg. 1 u. Sonne: kulturelles Vorwissen u. Erfahrungen der Kinder einbeziehen
Aufg. Sonne: Texte zu besonderen Festen verschriftlichen

Special days: Earth Day

1 Talk about the pictures. What is beautiful? What is bad?

animals • bad air • bees • birds • cars • Earth • fire • flowers • mountains • plastic (bottles / bags) • river • sea • sun • trees

1

2

3

4

5

6

2 Read and talk about the posters.

What can YOU do to keep the Earth green?
Make your own poster.
Think. → Pair. → Share.

3 When is Earth Day? Go on the internet. Type in "Earth Day".

Aufg. 1: *there's / there are* für die Bildbeschreibung nutzen
Aufg. Sonne: auf *Pupil's-Book*-Seite 25 verweisen
Aufg. 3: weiterführende Internet-Recherche zu „*Earth Day song / books for children*"

1 Make your own Easter bunny.

You need:

1 piece of square paper

scissors

Fold and cut the paper:

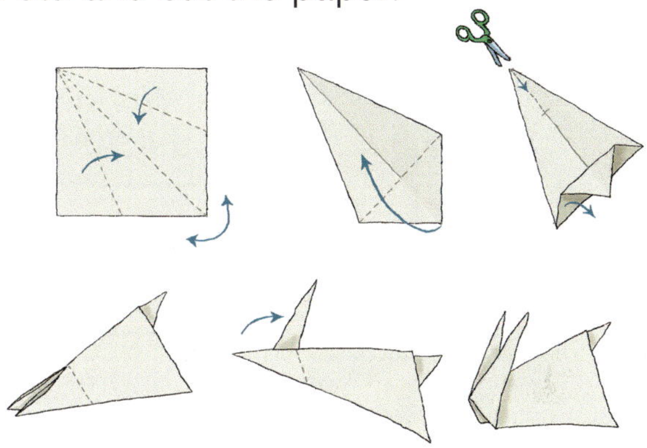

2 Listen to the Easter rhyme.

88

3 Say the rhyme.

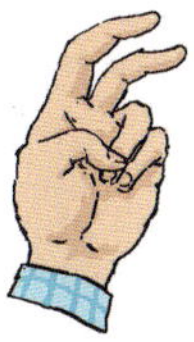

Here's a bunny
with ears so funny,

and here is his hole in the ground.

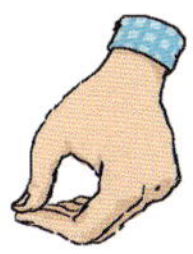

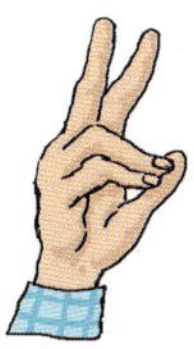

And when a noise he hears,
he pricks up his ears,

and hops in his hole in the ground.

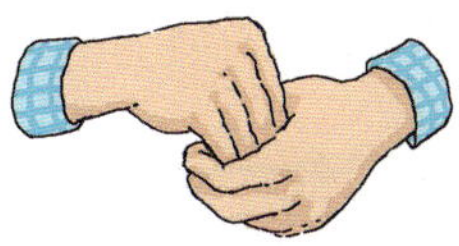

Note

In England essen die Menschen zu Ostern *hot cross buns.*

Was isst du gerne zu Ostern?

I like hot cross buns.
What do you like
for Easter?

Aufg. 3: Reim mit passenden Bewegungen unterstützen, s. Abb.

p. 60, 61 APP

Special days: Children's Day

① Look at the pictures. Talk.

There's ...

There are ...

② Read the texts. Point to the pictures.

Ⓐ

① It is World Children's Day every year on the 20th of November.

Ⓑ

② On World Children's Day, we celebrate children's rights – all children are wonderful!

Ⓒ

③ In Japan this day is called 'Kodomo no hi'. Families make a kite together, the 'koi nobori'.

Ⓓ

④ Some children of the world are not happy because they are ill or have to work. This is unfair.

③ Read the slogans. Explain.

④ Make a Children's Day bunting with one or more of the slogans.
Think. → Pair. → Share.

 APP p. 62, 63

Aufg. 1 u. 2: 20. November = internationaler Tag der Kinderrechte der UN; Datum in vielen Ländern abweichend
Aufg. 4: alternativ Poster anfertigen

Looking at English

So kannst du über dich und andere sprechen:

I am

you are

he is

she is

it is

we are

you are

they are

Manche Wörter werden abgekürzt:

(to) be (= sein):

I **am**	= I**'m**	we are	= we**'re**
you **are**	= you**'re**	you are	= you**'re**
he **is**	= he**'s**	they are	= they**'re**
she **is**	= she**'s**		
it **is**	= it**'s**		

I am = I'm

I am *verwendest du, wenn du etwas aufschreibst.*

I'm *verwendest du, wenn du etwas sagst.*

Weitere Kurzformen:

what is	= what**'s**	it is not	= it **isn't**	I have got	= I**'ve** got
where is	= where**'s**	they are not	= they **aren't**	she has got	= she**'s** got
that is	= that**'s**	I cannot	= I **can't**	I would like	= I**'d** like
there is	= there**'s**	I do not	= I **don't**	I will	= I**'ll**

So sagst du, dass jemandem etwas gehört:

This is Tim**'s** book.

This is **my** book.

This is Anne**'s** pencil case.

This is **my** pencil case.

Looking at English

So verändern sich die Wörter in der Mehrzahl:

① Wenn du von mehreren Dingen sprichst, hängst du ein „s“ an.

one apple – two apple**s**
one book – two book**s**

② Bei manchen Wörtern ändert sich die Schreibweise:

one cherry – two cherr**ies**
one tomato – two tomato**es**

③ Es gibt Ausnahmen, die du dir merken musst, z. B.:

one child – two child**ren**
one mouse – two **mice**

one fish – two **fish**
one reindeer – two **reindeer**

So kannst du über spontane Entscheidungen sprechen:

I'm cold.
I'll put on my jacket!

I'm hot.
I'll take off my coat!

So kannst du sagen, was du gerne machst:

I like **football.**

I like **playing football.**

So kannst du beschreiben, was jemand (auf einem Bild) gerade macht:

Samir **is dancing.**

Look! Harry and Emily **are playing** football.

Getting started

Numbers

1 one	4 four	7 seven	10 ten
2 two	5 five	8 eight	11 eleven
3 three	6 six	9 nine	12 twelve

am (→ to be)	bin	*I **am** nine years old.*
ball	Ball	
(to) be: am, are, is	sein: bin, bist, ist	*I **am** / You **are** / She **is** nine years old.*
bike	Fahrrad	
book	Buch	
cap	Kappe, Schirmmütze	
computer	Computer	
cornflakes	Cornflakes	
cowboy	Cowboy	
frisbee	Frisbee	
game	Spiel	
hamburger	Hamburger	
here	hier	
in-line skates	Inlineskates	
is (→ to be)	ist	*He **is** eight years old.*
jeans	Jeans	
laptop	Laptop	*There's a **laptop** in the toy shop.*
mole	Maulwurf	
Mr ...	Herr ... *(Anrede)*	*Good morning, **Mr** Green!*
Ms ...	Frau ... *(Anrede)*	
name	Name	*My **name** is Mr Mole.*
plane	Flugzeug	
popcorn	Popcorn	
puzzle	Puzzle	
sandwich	Sandwich	
scooter	Roller	

Word list für Deutsch – Englisch und Englisch – Deutsch (s. UMA)

Word list

skateboard	Skateboard	
smartphone	Smartphone	
smoothie	Smoothie	
T-shirt	T-Shirt	*There is one **T-shirt**.*
tablet	Tablet	*There are two **tablets**.*
toast	Toast	

Meeting friends

are (→ to be)	bist / sind / seid	*How old **are** you?*
aunt	Tante	
black	schwarz	
blue	blau	
baby	Baby	
brother	Bruder	*Have you got a **brother**?*
brown	braun	
(to) colour (in)	ausmalen	
colour	Farbe	
(to) come	kommen	*Can I **come** to your party?*
cousin	Cousin, Cousine	
dad	Papa	
family	Familie	*This is my **family**.*
father	Vater	
favourite	Lieblings-	
friend	Freund, Freundin	*Lucy is my **friend**.*
(front) door	Haustür, Tür	
grandfather	Großvater	
grandma	Oma	
grandmother	Großmutter	
grandpa	Opa	
green	grün	
grey	grau	
he	er	***He** is my friend.*
hopscotch	Himmel und Hölle *(Hüpfspiel)*	
house	Haus	
house number	Hausnummer	

it	er, sie, es	*Number 8 is Harry's door.* ***It****'s green.*
mother	Mutter	
mum	Mama	
number	Nummer	
O	Null *(in Telefonnummern)*	*My telephone number is five-***O***-...*
orange	orange	
pink	pink, rosa	
purple	lila	
red	rot	
she	sie	
sister	Schwester	*I have got a* ***sister****.*
telephone number	Telefonnummer	*What's your* ***telephone number****?*
uncle	Onkel	
white	weiß	
yellow	gelb	*My T-shirt is* ***yellow****.*

Pets in the garden

apple	Apfel	
bread	Brot	
budgie	Wellensittich	
can / can't	können / nicht können	*I* ***can*** *feed my pets.*
carrot	Möhre	
cat	Katze	
dice	Würfel	*Roll the* ***dice****.*
dog	Hund	
(to) eat	essen	
(to) feed	füttern	
fish	Fisch	
food	Essen *(Lebensmittel)*, Futter	
frog	Frosch	
garden shed	Gartenhaus	
(to) go	gehen	***Go*** *three steps forward.*
guinea pig	Meerschweinchen	
hamster	Hamster	
lettuce	Kopfsalat	*Guinea pigs like* ***lettuce****.*

Word list

(to) like	mögen	
mouse	Maus	
peanuts	Erdnüsse	
pet	Haustier	
(to) play	spielen	*Do you want to **play** hopscotch?*
rabbit	Kaninchen	
rat	Ratte	
tomato, tomatoes	Tomate, Tomaten	*I like **tomatoes**.*
tortoise	(Land-)Schildkröte	

At school

behind	hinter	
between	zwischen	*Emily is **between** Samir and Kate.*
book	Buch	
(to) colour (in)	ausmalen	
coloured pencil	Buntstift	*Have you got a **coloured pencil**?*
(to) draw	zeichnen	
felt tip	Filzstift	
(to) give	geben	***Give** it back, Jack!*
glue stick	Klebestift	
in	in	*The mouse is **in** the pencil case.*
in front of	vor *(räumlich)*	*The chair is **in front of** the table.*
(to) listen to	zuhören	*Please, **listen to** your teacher!*
lunch	Mittagessen	*It's time for **lunch**!*
lunch box	Brotdose	
next to	neben	
on	auf	
page	Seite	*Open your books at **page** 10.*
pen	Füller	
pencil	Bleistift	
pencil case	Federmäppchen	
pencil sharpener	Bleistiftspitzer	
pupil	Schüler, Schülerin	*There are 15 **pupils** and two teachers in the classroom.*
(to) put	(etwas wohin) legen, stellen, tun	***Put** the scissors on the table, please.*

(to) read	lesen	
rubber	Radiergummi	
ruler	Lineal	
school	Schule	
school bag	Schulranzen	
school things	Schulsachen	
scissors	Schere	*The **scissors** are in the pencil case.*
(to) take	nehmen	
(to) talk about something	über etwas sprechen	***Talk** about the picture.*
(to) talk to someone	mit jemandem sprechen	***Talk** to your partner.*
teacher	Lehrer, Lehrerin	
text	Text	
under	unter	
(to) write	schreiben	

At the second-hand shop

arm	Arm	
big	groß	
boots	Stiefel	*There are two pairs of **boots**.*
boy	Junge	
cardigan	Strickjacke	
clothes	Kleidung	
coat	Mantel	
cold	kalt	*I'm **cold**.*
colourful	bunt	
(to) design something	etwas designen / entwerfen	*This T-shirt is boring. I'll **design** a new look!*
dress	Kleid	
(to) dress	sich anziehen	
feet	Füße	
funny	lustig	
(to) find information	Informationen suchen / finden	
girl	Mädchen	
(to) give advice	Tipps geben	

Word list

gloves	Handschuhe	*It's cold outside. I'll put on my yellow **gloves**.*
hand	Hand	
hat	Mütze, Hut	
hot	heiß	
jacket	Jacke	
leg	Bein	
outfit	Outfit	
outside	draußen	
perfect	perfekt	*That's **perfect** for you!*
pullover	Pullover	
(to) put something on	etwas anziehen	*Tom, **put on** your jacket!*
right	richtig	
sandals	Sandalen	
scarf	Schal	
shirt	Hemd	
shoes	Schuhe	
shop assistant	Verkäufer	
shorts	Shorts, kurze Hose	
skirt	Rock	
small	klein	
so	daher, deshalb	*I like green – **so** I'll colour my T-shirt green!*
so boring	so langweilig	*The white T-shirt is **so boring**!*
socks	Socken	
something	etwas	
sunglasses	Sonnenbrille	*I love my new **sunglasses**!*
sunhat	Sonnenhut	
(to) take something off	etwas ausziehen	***Take off** your coat, Hannah.*
tie	Krawatte	
too big / small	zu groß / klein	*My pullover is **too small**.*
trainers	Turnschuhe	
trousers	Hose	
(to) type something in	etwas eintippen	
warm	warm	
(to) wear something	etwas anhaben	*I'm **wearing** my favourite outfit today.*

website	Internetseite, Website	
wrong	falsch	

Free-time activities

attic	Dachboden	
bathroom	Badezimmer	
bed	Bett	
bedroom	Schlafzimmer	
bookshelf, bookshelves	Bücherregal, Bücherregale	*There is a **bookshelf** in the classroom.* 
boring	langweilig	*Drawing pictures is **boring**.*
bugs	Ungeziefer	
chair	Stuhl	
(to) clean up	aufräumen	*What about **cleaning up** your bedroom?*
computer game	Computerspiel	
(to) dance	tanzen	*I like **dancing**.* 
desk	Schreibtisch	
(to) draw	zeichnen	*Look, Samir is **drawing** a picture.*
floor	Fußboden	
football	Fußball	*I like playing **football**.*
furniture	Möbel	
guitar	Gitarre	
hall	Diele	
hide-and-seek	Versteckspiel	*I like playing **hide-and-seek**.*
hobby, hobbies	Hobby, Hobbys	*What's your favourite **hobby**?*
kitchen	Küche	
music	Musik	
lamp	Lampe	
(to) like	mögen	*I **like** reading.* 
(to) listen to	zu-, anhören	*I like **listening to** music.*
living room	Wohnzimmer	
(to) meet	(sich) treffen	*I like **meeting** friends.*
picture	Bild	
(to) play	spielen	*I like **playing** the guitar.*
(to) read	lesen	
(to) ride a bike	Fahrrad fahren	*I like **riding** my bike.*

A-Z

Word list

room	Zimmer	
sofa	Sofa	
spider	Spinne	***Spiders*** *are helpful.*
stairs	Treppe, Treppenstufen	
table	Tisch	
toilet	Toilette	
wardrobe	Kleiderschrank	
(to) watch TV	fernsehen	

In the park

Numbers

20 **twenty**
30 **thirty**
40 **forty**
50 **fifty**
60 **sixty**
70 **seventy**
80 **eighty**
90 **ninety**
100 **one hundred**

apple	Apfel	*How much are the* ***apples****?*
avocado, avocadoes	Avocado, Avocados	
banana	Banane	
blueberry, blueberries	Blaubeere, Blaubeeren	*I like* ***blueberries****.*
cherry, cherries	Kirsche, Kirschen	
chocolate	Schokolade	
cucumber	Gurke	
(to) drink	trinken	
drink	Getränk	
grass	Gras	
hungry	hungrig	*I'm* ***hungry****.*
ice cream	Eiscreme	*My favourite* ***ice cream*** *is chocolate ice cream.*
juice	Saft	
kiwi	Kiwi	
lemon	Zitrone	*What about some* ***lemon*** *ice cream?*
mango, mangoes	Mango, Mangos	

milk	Milch	
orange	Orange	*Do you like* ***orange*** *juice?*
park	Park	*Let's have a picnic in the* ***park****.*
peach, peaches	Pfirsich, Pfirsiche	
pear	Birne	
pence (p)	Penny *(britische Währung)*	*The bananas are 80* ***pence / p****.*
pepper	Paprika	
pineapple	Ananas	
plum	Pflaume	
pound (£)	Pfund *(britische Währung)*	*That's 2* ***pounds****, please.*
raspberry, raspberries	Himbeere, Himbeeren	
smoothie	Smoothie	*Can I have a banana* ***smoothie****, please?*
snack	Snack	
spinach	Spinat	
strawberry, strawberries	Erdbeere, Erdbeeren	*What about some* ***strawberries****?*
thirsty	durstig	*I'm* ***thirsty****.*
tree	Baum	
vanilla	Vanille	
water	Wasser	

Special days: Birthday

January Januar	**April** April	**July** Juli	**October** Oktober
February Februar	**May** Mai	**August** August	**November** November
March März	**June** Juni	**September** September	**December** Dezember

birthday	Geburtstag	*My birthday is in* ***January****.* *My birthday is on 24th* ***February****.*
birthday card	Grußkarte zum Geburtstag	
(to) celebrate	feiern	*Let's* ***celebrate****!*
invitation card	Einladungskarte	

Word list

party	Party	*Have a nice* ***party****!*
present	Geschenk	*I love my* ***presents****!*

Special days: Christmas

bell	Glocke	
(to) celebrate	feiern	*We (don't)* ***celebrate*** *Christmas.*
chimney	Kamin	
Christmas	Weihnachten	
Christmas card	Grußkarte zu Weihnachten	
Christmas cracker	Knallbonbon	
Christmas Day	Weihnachtstag (25.12.)	
Christmas Eve	Heiligabend (24.12.)	
Christmas tree	Weihnachtsbaum	*Many people put presents under the* ***Christmas tree****.*
Father Christmas (British) / Santa Claus (USA)	Weihnachtsmann	
(to) go to church / mosque / synagogue	in die Kirche / Moschee / Synagoge gehen	
present	Geschenk	*Children love to get* ***presents*** *for Christmas.*
reindeer	das Rentier / die Rentiere	*The* ***reindeer*** *are coming.*
roof	Dach	*I hear them on the* ***roof****!*
(to) stay at home	zuhause bleiben	
stockings	Strümpfe	
(to) visit	besuchen	*We* ***visit*** *family and friends on Christmas.*
wish list	Wunschliste	

Special days: Earth Day

air	Luft	
animal	Tier	*I like wild* ***animals****!*
bad	schlecht	
bag	Tasche, Tüte	
beautiful	schön	*The Earth is so* ***beautiful****!*
bee	Biene	
bird	Vogel	

bottle	Flasche	*Say 'No!' to plastic **bottles** and plastic bags!*
car	Auto	
clean	sauber	
Earth	Erde *(Planet)*	
fire	Feuer	
flower	Blume	*The **flowers** smell fantastic!* 
mountain	Berg	
plastic	Plastik	***Plastic** in nature is bad.*
(to) recycle	recyceln	
river	Fluss	
sea	Meer	*Let's keep rivers and the **sea** clean!*
sky	Himmel	
sun	Sonne	
(to) take care of ...	sich um ... kümmern	
tree	Baum	
(to) walk	zu Fuß gehen	***Walk** to school or ride your bike.*
(to) waste	verschwenden	*Don't **waste** water.*

Special days: Easter

chocolate	Schokolade	
Easter	Ostern	
Easter basket	Osterkorb	
Easter bunny	Osterhase	*The **Easter bunny** hops in his hole in the ground.*
Easter egg	Osterei	*Harry has got some colourful **Easter eggs** in his Easter basket.* 
Easter Sunday	Ostersonntag	
egg hunt	Eiersuche	*Let's go on an an **egg hunt** on Easter Sunday.*

Word list

Special days: Children's Day

bunting	Wimpelkette	
(to) celebrate	feiern	
(to) collect litter	Müll sammeln	
dangerous	gefährlich	
every	jede, jeder, jedes	***Every*** *year on 20th November it is World Children's Day.*
happy	glücklich, froh	*Playing with my dog makes me* ***happy****.*
happiness	Glück, Freude	
(to) have friends	Freunde haben	*Children love* ***having friends****.*
ill	krank	*Some children are* ***ill****.*
kite	Drachen	*Children in Japan make a* ***kite*** *for Children's Day.*
(to) learn	lernen	
(to) live in peace	in Frieden leben	***Living in peace*** *is a right for everybody.*
nature	Natur	*Plastic is bad for our* ***nature****!*
playground	Spielplatz	
rights	Rechte	*Children have* ***rights****, too.*
sad	traurig	
(to) save (water)	(Wasser) sparen	
stripe	Streifen	*Cut out* ***stripes****.* 
wonderful	wundervoll	*Children are* ***wonderful****.*
World Children's Day	Weltkindertag	